Published in 2020 by Struik Lifestyle
an imprint of Penguin Random House South Africa (Pty) Ltd
Company Reg. No. 1953/000441/07
The Estuaries, 4 Oxbow Crescent, Century Avenue,
Century City 7441, Cape Town, South Africa
PO Box 1144, Cape Town, 8000, South Africa
www.penguinrandomhouse.co.za

ISBN 978-1-43231-037-0

PUBLISHER: Beverley Dodd
MANAGING EDITOR: Cecilia Barfield
CONCEPT & COVER DESIGNER: Marina Grieves
TYPESETTER: Randall Watson
PROOFREADER: Gill Gordon
PHOTOGRAPHERS: See backcover flap

Reproduction by Hirt & Carter Cape (Pty) Ltd & Studio Repro
Printed and bound in China by RR Donnelley

Penguin Random House is committed to a sustainable
future for our business, our readers and our planet.
This book is made from Forest Stewardship Council®
certified paper.

Out of an AFRICAN KITCHEN

A quirky anthology of recipes, reminiscences, anecdotes and stories from a bush kitchen set high up on the edge of the Great Rift Valley, overlooking Kenya's lovely Maasai Mara Game Reserve.

Dedication

This book is written in honour of the chefs at Angama Mara and our guests who, over the past five years, have made this dream possible.

CONTENTS

OUR STORY

Our food is good. Our food is not fancy.

How can you possibly feed guests who, when not on safari, eat in the best restaurants on the planet?

We nervously asked ourselves this question as we prepared to open Angama Mara in 2015. It is a daunting challenge to prepare food in the middle of nowhere for guests who come from all four corners of the world, from different culinary cultures and who (quite rightly) expect the best of the best when it comes to choosing where to stay for their next holiday.

Having fed guests on safari on two continents and across seven countries for the past 25 years, I had an inkling that, for our guests, less is preferable to more. Certainly not less food, as we love feeding them as many times a day as they will allow us. Less fiddle, more authenticity. Less fancy imported ingredients, more locally grown. Less drizzles, gels and foams, more wholesome and generous. Less drama on the plate, more drama where we serve our food. Less ego in the kitchen, more a love of seeing our guests happy at what we have prepared for them.

It didn't take long to find our North Star: our food would be good; our food would never be fancy.

And from there it was easy. Well, sort of. We gathered a team of Kenyan chefs, all of whom shared a great attitude and love of service. To their collective terror, they were told not one buffet. Ever. Only à la carte and we would serve our guests when and where they would like to eat and, if possible, whatever they would like to eat. We planned menus and designed kitchens and readied ourselves for our first guests. What we hadn't anticipated was having our kitchens commissioned only two days before opening. That, needless to add, caused tears, blood, drama, sweat and more tears.

We drew inspiration from the finest ingredients Kenya has to offer: beautiful vegetables from the highlands, tropical fruits a-plenty from the coast, cheese from a renowned supplier just outside Nairobi, prawns from Malindi, freshwater fish from Lake Victoria and beef from the north. And you will discover, as you read this book, that Kenyan cuisine is deeply influenced by Arab-inspired Swahili dishes from the coast and Indian food from the significant community that has called this country home for many generations.

We debated what we could offer our guests that they couldn't find elsewhere and what they would remember most about Angama's food. We knew that not one Michelin-starred chef in the world could prepare picnics served under a lone tree in the middle of the short grass plains of the Maasai Mara with only giraffe, elephant and buffalo as dining companions. We planted a beautiful one-acre kitchen garden, our Shamba, where guests could pick their own vegetables and toss their own salads for lunch. In the evenings, they would dine in a lantern-lit forest off a barbecue à la carte menu with the calls of hyena serenading them as they shared stories of their day's adventures on safari.

Five years on and we are still learning, still making mistakes and still improving in the kitchen. I am so proud of the team. Nothing is ever too much trouble. Gluten free? Easy. Vegan? No problem. Low sodium, kosher, no garlic, Chinese, food allergies, Halaal and food preferences are all in a day's work. The children only like fish fingers. Done. Soy milk, almond milk? In the pantry. Do we get it right all of the time? No, but the vast majority of our guests tuck into our Best Burger in the Mara with relish. They appreciate that our food is honest, fresh and, most of all, prepared and cooked with love. And also served with love. Our merry band of gracious butlers have had to learn that paneer is not penne and tagliatelle is not tagliata and what are harissa, sumac and za'atar?

Often our guests ask the chefs for a recipe and of course we print or email whatever they want. The next logical step was why not write a cookbook for our guests? And so this book was born. Each of the recipes is drawn from our daily menus and many of these dishes are inspired by some of the world's best-loved chefs: Yotam, Heston, Danny and more. They lead, we follow.

A heartfelt 'thank you' to our guests for coming to stay with us and a heartfelt 'thank you' to the chefs of the Angama kitchens for all they do every day to ensure that our guests are never hungry, never disappointed and always delighted.

Nicky Fitzgerald

Founder and owner

OUR GOOD NEIGHBOURS

Guests often ask us how we get our fresh produce here, in the middle of nowhere. We are tempted to answer, 'as if by magic', but the truth is we order the finest ingredients from Nairobi, fresh seafood from the coast, and Kenya's famed beef from the north. But peskier products, like sumac and black quinoa, come from South Africa. After all, how could our guests survive without sumac and black quinoa?

But our best suppliers are neighbours and friends from the heart of Maasailand. A few times a week, farmer Joseph Oseko putters into camp on his small motorbike, laden with sacks of cabbages, kale, tomatoes, bananas, onions, watermelons and the biggest, most delicious avocados under the sun. How he fits it all on the back of his bike is nothing short of a miracle. At our Forest Barbecue, we serve Joseph's avocados whole and guests not only devour them, but sneak them back to their tents to take to their next destination.

Maasailand is the land of milk and honey. Julius Mokita, another neighbour, works with a collective of Maasai beekeepers and honey producers from villages surrounding our lodge. They combine their 100 per cent-organic honey with a lovely smoky flavour, producing enough to supply lodges around the Mara, all delivered in five-litre buckets swinging on the handlebars of a motorbike. Maasai honey is the hero in two recipes in this book: a classical Kenyan cocktail, the Dawa, and our much-loved Maasai Honey Biscuits.

The whole Angama team is fuelled by Kenya's famous chai – tea stewed with fresh cow's milk and heaps of sugar – an acquired taste enjoyed by more and more of our guests. The mother of our storekeeper, Joshua, delivers fresh milk daily for 4 o'clock tea. That's five litres every day, rain or shine, and Mama Joshua walks from her manyatta to the lodge. To prepare 25 litres of Kenyan chai, you need 15 litres unpasteurized milk, 10 litres water, 200g tea leaves and 2.5kg sugar. Pour the milk into a large pot, bring to the boil, add the water and bring back to the boil. Add the tea leaves and sugar and boil until the tea turns brown. Sieve into a very large kettle ready to serve.

AT THE LODGE

Suspended in mid air

Could there be a more lovely setting for a pre-safari breakfast than on the edge of the Great Rift Valley? Guests watch hot air balloons floating dreamily by while enjoying a cappuccino brewed from Kenyan coffee beans.

A great view, warm service and delicious food – what could be better? Breakfast, lunch and dinner are served on the decks that wrap across the front of Angama's guest areas. And if you look down into the reserve, 300 metres below, you will see graceful giraffe journeying across the open grasslands, a family of elephant slowly making their daily trek from the forests that surround us to the lush marshes below, and, of course, there is that family of buffalo, 100 strong, who on a good day might move from one side of the road to another. Look out, not up, and there are always raptors sailing past at eye level, almost close enough to touch.

But the food has to match the setting and we have chosen five of our best-loved dishes to share with you in this chapter. The Best Burger in the Mara is our guests' favourite. Why is it the best? Probably because we are the only lodge that serves them every single day of the year. That's how much our guests love them. Who would have thought?

GAZPACHO WITH OLIVE TAPENADE

GAZPACHO

SHOP IT

2 ½ cups diced cucumber

1 cup diced red pepper

2 cups diced ripe tomatoes

½ cup diced red onion

4 cloves garlic

2 cups tomato juice

⅓ cup olive oil

2 tsp sugar

2 dashes Worcestershire Sauce

salt and freshly ground black pepper to taste

PREPARE IT

Blend all the ingredients together and chill.

Garnish the soup with a generous blob of tapenade and a swirl of good olive oil.

Serves 1

OLIVE TAPENADE

SHOP IT

1 cup pitted black olives

2 Tbsp capers

2 cloves garlic

¼ tsp chilli flakes

½ cup fresh basil

½ cup fresh parsley

2 Tbsp olive oil

PREPARE IT

Blend all the ingredients in a food processor until smooth. Refrigerate until ready to use. Will keep for up to a week.

Chef Evans makes all our soups using a good vegetable stock. As he says, 'We need to look after our vegetarian guests.'

SPICY PRAWN SUSHI STACK WITH PICKLED GINGER & CARROT SLAW

Shannon is Angama Mara's regional director and is responsible for the smooth operation of our kitchens. Homesick for far-off Seattle and sushi, she introduced 'The Stack' to our lunch menu.

SPICY PRAWN SUSHI STACK

SHOP IT

1 cup sushi rice

2 Tbsp rice wine vinegar

2 Tbsp sugar

1 Tbsp salt

½ cup soy sauce

2 tsp honey

2 tsp fresh minced ginger

a small bunch of chives, chopped

¼ cup finely diced cucumber

4 Tbsp mayonnaise

1 Tbsp chilli sauce (your favourite)

¼ cup cooked prawns, peeled, tails removed and diced

2 Tbsp mashed avocado

1 tsp sesame seeds, toasted (black or white or a combination)

PREPARE IT

Cook the rice according to packet instructions and transfer to a bowl. Combine rice wine vinegar, sugar and salt in small bowl and microwave for 30–45 seconds. Add the vinegar mixture to the rice and mix thoroughly. Allow to cool to room temperature before making the sushi stack.

Make a dipping sauce by whisking together the soy sauce, honey and ginger.

To assemble, combine the chives and cucumbers in a small bowl. Combine the mayonnaise and chilli sauce and toss in the prawns. Place a lightly oiled metal ring on a plate. Cover the bottom with the sushi rice and cover with a layer of the prawn mixture. Add the avocado to cover the prawns, about 1cm thick. Finally, top with the cucumber-chive mixture. Do not press into sides of the ring. Carefully remove the metal ring. Sprinkle with the toasted sesame seeds. Serve with the dipping sauce and Pickled Ginger & Carrot Slaw.

Serves 1

PICKLED GINGER & CARROT SLAW

SHOP IT

3 knobs unpeeled fresh ginger, scrubbed and thinly sliced

1 cup white vinegar

1 ½ tsp sea salt

3 tsp sugar

1 cup water

2 medium carrots, peeled, sliced into ribbons and finely julienned

PREPARE IT

Combine the ginger, vinegar, salt, sugar and water in a small saucepan, then bring to a boil over medium-high heat. Keep stirring with a wooden spoon until the sugar and salt have dissolved. Remove from the heat. Strain the ginger brine through a sieve into a heatproof bowl. Slice the ginger into fine julienne strips and add the carrots. Pour the brine over, making sure everything is fully immersed. Cover and cool to room temperature. Transfer to a clean jar, seal tightly with a lid and refrigerate for up to 2 weeks.

ASPARAGUS WITH PARMESAN-CRUSTED BOILED EGG & BUTTER SAUCE

We have drawn inspiration, borrowed, reinvented and copied delicious dishes from friends across the world. This recipe was created by Kathy Romer-Lee of Oaklands Country Manor in the Drakensberg region of South Africa. Next time you are driving from Johannesburg to Durban, be sure to stay over – Kathy's pork belly dish is legendary.

SHOP IT

350g medium asparagus spears

4 large eggs

3 Tbsp seasoned flour

1 egg, beaten

½ cup fresh breadcrumbs and finely grated parmesan cheese (in equal quantities)

½ cup melted salted butter

2 Tbsp snipped fresh chives

4 lemon cheeks

salt and freshly ground black pepper

PREPARE IT

Wash the asparagus spears well and trim them to the same length.

Boil the 4 large eggs in salted water for 5 minutes. Remove from the pot and immediately plunge them into iced water. Leave to cool for 5 minutes then peel (using a teaspoon to assist if necessary). Dip the peeled eggs gently into seasoned flour, then beaten egg, followed by the breadcrumb-parmesan mixture. Deep-fry the eggs over a moderate heat until golden.

Just before serving, quickly cook the asparagus in boiling salted water until tender. Divide the asparagus among four plates and arrange on each in a bunch. Gently spoon the melted butter over the asparagus and sprinkle with the chives. Cut the boiled eggs in half and place on the asparagus. Season to taste. Serve with a lemon cheek on the side.

Serves 4

KITCHEN NOTE

The size and altitude affects the softness of the egg. It's a good idea to boil one egg first to see if it is perfect before cooking all the eggs.

BEST BURGER IN THE MARA

The 'smashed burger' was made famous by Danny Meyer's Shake Shack. We love the crispy edges and the sauce so much we simply had to model ours on his. A touch of New York City in the Mara.

SHOP IT

500g minced beef

2 Tbsp butter, plus more if needed

4 hamburger rolls, halved

2 Tbsp vegetable oil

salt and freshly ground black pepper to taste

2 tomatoes, cut into 1cm-thick slices

1 cup grated strong cheddar cheese

4 burger-sized lettuce leaves

2 large pickled gherkins, thinly sliced lengthways

Sauce:

¼ cup mayonnaise

1 ½ tsp pickle juice

1 ½ tsp ketchup or tomato sauce

1 tsp prepared mustard

¼ tsp smoked paprika

PREPARE IT

Shape the minced beef into 4 equal-sized, 6cm-thick flat balls or 'pucks'. Place these patties on a plate lined with waxed paper and freeze for 15 minutes. The meat must extra-cold but not frozen when it hits the pan.

To make the sauce, combine all the ingredients, check the flavour and make any adjustments if necessary.

Heat a cast-iron pan over medium heat. Melt the butter and place the rolls, cut-side down, in the pan. Toast for 1–2 minutes until the cut sides are golden-brown. Transfer the rolls to 4 plates. Remove the patties from the freezer. Increase the heat to high, add oil to the pan and heat until the oil begins to smoke (at least 2 minutes). Working one at a time, flatten each patty in the pan to a 2cm thickness, pressing hard to flatten. Generously season with salt and pepper. Once the patty is brown with crisp, scraggly edges (1½–2 minutes for medium), flip it over with a spatula to scrape underneath the meat. Repeat with the remaining patties.

Spoon some of the sauce over the bottom burger rolls. Transfer the cooked patties onto the rolls. Top with tomatoes, grated cheese, lettuce, pickles and the upper rolls.

Serve with potato wedges and battered onion rings, if you like.

Serves 4

TIRAMISINI WITH COFFEE ICE CREAM

After a lantern-lit barbecue in the forest, our guests return to camp to be greeted by a tiered display of Dessert Bitings. Bitings is a catchall description, originally from India, for small bites of food. Our guests can choose as many mouthfuls of desserts as they please.

TIRAMISINI

SHOP IT
16 ladyfinger biscuits

3 large eggs, separated

1/3 cup sugar

250ml mascarpone

1/3 cup marsala

1 cup strong, warm espresso coffee, sweetened with 1 Tbsp sugar

16 Tbsp grated dark chocolate

2 Tbsp cocoa powder, for sifting (optional)

PREPARE IT
In a medium bowl, beat the egg whites until stiff. In a larger bowl, beat the egg yolks, then add the sugar and continue beating for 3–4 minutes until thick and pale yellow. Mix in the mascarpone and beat for 1 minute for extra fluff. Beat in the marsala until smooth. Gently fold in the egg whites until combined (try not to deflate the mixture). It will be a loose, soft, creamy custard. Pour the sweetened espresso into a small bowl wide enough for dipping the biscuits.

To assemble in small cups, Moroccan tea glasses or martini glasses: dip a biscuit in espresso until almost fully saturated, but not falling apart. Halve the biscuit and place the first half in the bottom of the glass. Spoon a generous tablespoon of the cream mixture over it. Sprinkle with a tablespoon of chocolate. Repeat with the other half of the biscuit and another spoonful of mixture. Repeat this layering with a second biscuit which should be nearly at the top of the glass. Sprinkle with grated chocolate. Repeat with the remaining glasses.

Chill overnight to set. Before serving, dust with cocoa powder if using.

Serves 8 (depending on size of serving glass)

COFFEE ICE CREAM

SHOP IT
2 cups fresh cream

1 x 385g can sweetened condensed milk

8 egg whites

50ml strong cooled espresso coffee

PREPARE IT
Whip the cream until soft peaks form. Slowly add the condensed milk, mixing all the time.

In a separate bowl, beat the egg whites until soft peaks form, then carefully fold them into the cream and condensed milk mixture. Finally fold in the coffee. Churn in an ice cream machine until ready. Serve in scoops over the Tiramisini.

Serves 8

PROUDLY KENYAN

Swahili dreaming

The recorded history of Kenya dates back over 1000 years and its cuisine reflects its multicultural past. Sometime during the first millennium, Arab traders sailed their way south in dhows during the monsoon, kicking off a brisk trade with coastal inhabitants in ivory, gold, slaves and timber. Arab-Swahili states sprung up from Mozambique Island in the south to lovely Lamu in the north, and these important centres traded goods between the Kenyan interior and Arabia, Persia and China. Vasco da Gama sailed into Mombasa in 1498 and 200 years of Portuguese rule followed. The Omanis sent the Portuguese packing in 1730 and settled in until British rule replaced them in 1895.

The trade in slaves and ivory was, thankfully, replaced by trade in spices. Kenya's beautiful coastal areas are planted with cloves, cinnamon, cardamom, turmeric, cumin and coriander. Chillies, vanilla, all manner of spices, coconuts, tropical fruits and fresh fish in abundance still form the building blocks of Swahili cuisine up to the present. A significant influence on Kenyan cooking was brought by thousands of indentured labourers recruited from India between 1896 and 1901 to construct the Uganda Railway. Indian cuisine is served in some of the finest restaurants in the country to this day. But more of that in a later chapter.

KENYAN QUESADILLAS WITH GUACAMOLE

We love the Mexican-Kenyan crossover of this recipe using a local classic staple, the chapatti, as the hero for making the quesadillas. We first ate this dish in Nairobi's Afro-chic Nyama Mama restaurant and simply couldn't resist featuring it on our lunch menu.

QUESADILLAS

SHOP IT

2 onions, finely chopped

¹/₂ cup olive oil

1 ¹/₂ Tbsp ground cumin

3 cloves garlic, crushed

3 x 400g cans butter beans

1 ¹/₂ Tbsp sugar

6 thin chapattis (or large flour tortillas)

1 bunch spring onions, finely sliced

6 tomatoes, thinly sliced, seasoned with salt and pepper

¹/₄ cup plain yoghurt

4 mozzarella balls, halved and thinly sliced

PREPARE IT

Sauté the onions in olive oil until tender, but not brown. Add the cumin and garlic and cook for 2 minutes. Add the beans and sugar and fry while mashing the beans to a paste.

For the filling, spread one half of each chapatti with the refried beans, leaving a 1cm border. Scatter with the spring onions and tomato slices, enough to cover the beans. Top with 2 teaspoons of yoghurt each and slices of mozzarella. Fold the chapattis into half-moons and gently fry on both sides in a lightly oiled pan, until they take on a lovely golden colour and the mozzarella has melted.

Slice into 4 wedges, garnish as desired and serve with the Guacamole on the side.

Serves 6

GUACAMOLE

SHOP IT

2 avocados, pulp smashed with a fork

2 tomatoes, peeled, seeded and finely chopped

¹/₂ medium onion, finely chopped

¹/₂ bunch fresh coriander, finely chopped

¹/₂ chilli, finely chopped

2 Tbsp lemon juice

salt to taste

PREPARE IT

Mash all the ingredients together, adjust the seasoning and serve at room temperature.

Makes 3 cups

UGALI STICKS WITH HONEY-MUSTARD MAYO

SHOP IT

2 cups water

50g butter

¹⁄₂ cup milk

salt and pepper

*1 cup ugali (Kenyan maize flour)
   or polenta plus a little extra*

¹⁄₂ cup chopped fresh parsley

vegetable oil for deep frying

Honey-mustard mayo:

¹⁄₂ cup mayonnaise

2 Tbsp Dijon mustard

2 Tbsp honey

PREPARE IT

Bring the water to a boil, add the butter, milk, and salt and pepper to taste. Add the ugali (or polenta) and parsley. Mix well and bring back to a boil, stirring all the time to a thick but not dry consistency. Spread over a lightly oiled baking tray and allow to cool. Cut into 1.5cm-thick and 9cm-long fingers. Roll the fingers in more ugali or polenta and deep fry until crispy and golden.

Mix the mayonnaise, Dijon mustard and honey together, tasting to balance the flavours.

Serve the Ugali Sticks while still warm, with the Honey Mustard Mayo on the side.

Serves 6 as a snack

Chefs Musa and John stir up an ugali storm each day in our staff canteen kitchen.

SWAHILI RICE PUDDING WITH MANGO

SHOP IT

¾ cup soft brown sugar or jaggery

2 ½ litres milk

1 x 400ml can coconut milk

1 cup whipping cream

240g arborio rice

60g butter

½ cup soft brown sugar or jaggery

2 tsp vanilla essence

2 tsp freshly ground cardamom

1 large mango, peeled, pitted and diced for serving

fresh cream for serving

PREPARE IT

Start by making a caramel sauce in a heavy-bottomed saucepan, caramelise three-quarters of a cup of soft brown sugar or jaggery, adding a little water until it boils and becomes thick and syrupy. Set the caramel sauce aside.

Place all the other ingredients in a large, heavy pot and bring to a boil. Cook slowly, stirring occasionally to prevent the rice from sticking. When the rice is almost cooked, add extra sugar and cardamom if needed. Once the rice mixture has thickened and the rice is very soft, pour into serving glasses or bowls and allow to cool until a skin has formed.

Serve topped with the caramel sauce and diced fresh mangoes, and cream on the side.

Serves 8–10 (depending on size of glass or bowl)

Chef Katana, a maestro of Swahili cooking, is also known as 'The Man with the Palate'.

SWAHILI CHOCOLATE POTS WITH SESAME SHARDS

SWAHILI CHOCOLATE POTS

SHOP IT

250g dark chocolate, finely chopped

1 ½ Tbsp cornflour

450ml milk

1 cup cream

1 Tbsp vanilla essence

½ red chilli with seeds, halved lengthwise

chilli powder or cayenne pepper (optional)

5 egg yolks

1 ½ cups white sugar

whipped fresh cream for serving

PREPARE IT

Place the chocolate into a large heatproof bowl.

Mix the cornflour and a quarter cup of the milk together to form a paste.

In a large saucepan bring the remaining milk, cream, vanilla essence and chilli to a boil. Remove the chilli and taste. If not spicy enough, add chilli powder or cayenne pepper to taste. Stir in the cornflour mixture and gently boil until the mixture thickens slightly. Whisk the egg yolks and sugar together until light and fluffy. Slowly add the hot milk mixture to the eggs, beating well with each addition. Return the mixture to the pan and cook over a gentle heat until the custard starts to thicken. The custard should coat the back of a spoon. Whisk continuously while cooking to prevent the custard from curdling.

Remove from the heat and pour half the hot custard over the chocolate. Stir until melted and combined. Add the other half of the custard into the chocolate and mix well.

Pour into small glasses or ramekins and chill for at least 2 hours before serving. Serve with a blob of whipped cream and Sesame Shards. If you like, you could decorate with a whole chilli for added colour.

Serves 6–8 (depending on size of serving glass)

SESAME SHARDS

SHOP IT

2 cups castor sugar

8 Tbsp water

¾ cup white sesame seeds

PREPARE IT

Oil a baking tray with vegetable oil or use a silicone baking sheet rubbed with oil. Place the sugar and water in a heavy-based saucepan over a medium heat. Using a spoon, stir until it dissolves then stop stirring until it starts to caramelise into a light golden colour. Add the sesame seeds and continue cooking until dark golden. Take care not to burn the caramel.

Pour the caramel onto the prepared tray or baking sheet. Use an oiled palette knife, spread out to about 5mm thick (the thinner the caramel, the better). Allow the caramel to cool completely and then break up into shards.

Chef Kisimei agrees that chocolate and chilli is a marriage made in heaven.

SWAHILI MUHAMRI COCONUT ICE CREAM SANDWICH

Everyone loves fried dough: the Italians with their bomboloni; the French and beignets; koeksisters from South Africa; and jelebi from India, to name but a few. In Kenya we have two ways of frying dough, mandazi from the hinterland and the lighter, more elegant and utterly delicious muhamri from the coast.

SWAHILI MUHAMRI

SHOP IT

2 ½ cups cake flour

3 Tbsp sugar

1 tsp dry yeast

½ tsp roughly ground cardamom (freshly ground for best flavour)

½ cup coconut milk

warm water to bind

oil for deep frying

icing sugar for dusting

PREPARE IT

Combine the flour, sugar, yeast and cardamom in a bowl, then add the coconut milk and mix well. Add enough warm water to form a soft (but not sticky) dough and knead well. Place the dough in an oiled bowl, cover and leave in a warm place for 2-3 hours, until doubled in size. Knock down the dough, knead again and roll out to a thickness of 5mm. Using a plain pastry, round cutter, cut into portions. Leave for another 15 minutes to prove a second time.

Fry in hot oil until golden and puffed on both sides. Allow to cool.

To serve, split each muhamri in half, fill with the Coconut Ice Cream and generously dust with icing sugar.

Serves 12

COCONUT ICE CREAM

SHOP IT

2 cups fresh cream

1 x 400ml can coconut milk

1 x 385g can sweetened condensed milk

PREPARE IT

Whisk the cream until soft peaks form, then fold in the coconut milk and condensed milk. Freeze until ready to scoop into the muhamris.

IN THE SHAMBA

A magical place where unicorns roam

Inspired by the magnificent eight-acre, formal kitchen garden at Babylonstoren in the Cape winelands in South Africa, we thought, 'Why not plant a kitchen garden in Maasailand?'. Unlike our garden muse to the south, we had to take a more robust approach: how do we keep the elephants out; eland are known to clear five-metre-high fences in search of good food; porcupines can burrow under virtually any impediment; baboons have to be chased off (tiresome but doable); but what we hadn't considered as our biggest thief turned out to be the nondescript speckled mousebird. When you visit our lovely shamba – the Swahili word for kitchen garden – whatever you do, don't mention that bird.

Our extended Angama family covers every talent we require, so in no time Ian Dommisse (brother of our digital marketing manager, Alison) landed in the Mara. Ian is best described as an architect-gone-green. The brief was simple: design a magical garden that first and foremost will delight our guests, and in which the shamba keepers will grow all the beautiful salads, herbs and finer vegetables used in our kitchen. We pegged out the one acre needed (no trees disturbed), built and grew the fortifications (think Sleeping Beauty's thorn fortress) and laid out the garden that overlooks the Mara below. In just two years the shamba was flourishing and, to date, we have only had one massive elephant raid (beetroot, bananas, sweetcorn and mangoes on the menu that day).

Many of our guests choose to have lunch in the shamba, and our only proviso is that they harvest their own salads (using gold secateurs, of course). It has become a much-loved experience at Angama Mara, although we are still searching for ways to keep those birds away. And the unicorn? The area surrounding the shamba is the territory of a handsome one-horned waterbuck. Naturally.

VANILLA ALMOND FRENCH TOAST WITH PASSIONFRUIT & MANGO

SHOP IT

2 eggs

2 Tbsp sugar

2 tsp vanilla essence

a pinch of salt

¾ cup milk

½ cup almonds, coarsely chopped

2 Tbsp butter

4 slices white bread (preferably challah or brioche)

4 passionfruit, pulp scooped out

1 large mango, peeled, pitted and cubed

200g mascarpone for serving

PREPARE IT

In a shallow dish, whisk together the eggs, sugar, vanilla essence and salt. Then whisk in the milk. Lightly brown the almonds in the butter in a frying pan. Meanwhile, soak the bread in the milk mixture.

Place the bread on top of the almonds in the pan and cook until both almonds and bread turn golden-brown (about 3 minutes each side).

To serve, cut the bread in half diagonally (if you like), top with fresh fruit, and a side serving of mascarpone cheese.

Serves 4

KITCHEN NOTE

Any or all of the following fruits work well: mango, papaya, passionfruit, banana and strawberries.

Shamba-keeper Naliki not only has the greenest of fingers and is a master of honey harvesting, but he is also determined to find the solution to keeping the speckled mousebirds out of his garden.

GREEN SHAKSHUKA
WITH OLIVE OIL CRACKERS

GREEN SHAKSHUKA

SHOP IT

½ tsp caraway seeds

3 medium bunches green spinach

2 green chillies, seeds removed and finely chopped

½ cup coriander leaves

1 tsp ground cumin

1 cup ice

½ cup plus 2 Tbsp olive oil

1 large onion, sliced

salt and freshly ground black pepper

16 large eggs

Sumac and coarsely chopped dill to taste

PREPARE IT

Toast the caraway seeds in a small dry pan over medium heat, tossing often, until fragrant, about 1 minute. Leave to cool; then finely grind in mortar and pestle.

Remove the ribs and stems from 1 bunch of spinach. Blanch the leaves in a large pot of salted boiling water for 10 seconds. Immediately transfer to a bowl of iced water. Drain and squeeze out any excess water. Coarsely chop and transfer to a blender. Add the chillies, coriander, cumin, ground caraway seeds, a half cup of oil and the ice. Purée, adding more ice if needed, until smooth. Season with salt. Remove the ribs and stems from the remaining spinach. Tear the leaves into bite-size pieces. Heat the remaining 2 tablespoons of oil in a large frying pan and cook the onion until soft. Add the spinach leaves, salt and pepper, and cook until the spinach wilts. Add the purée and mix well. Spoon the mixture into 8 individual baking dishes, make 2 dents in the top of each and break the eggs into the dents. Sprinkle lightly with salt and sumac. Cook* until the eggs are just set. Scatter with dill to serve.

Serves 8

KITCHEN NOTE*

This dish can be cooked in a 180°C oven until eggs reach their desired firmness or on top of the stove and finished under the grill.

OLIVE OIL CRACKERS

SHOP IT

250g flour

1 tsp baking powder

150ml water

25ml olive oil

½ tsp salt

1 tsp paprika

¼ tsp cayenne pepper

¼ tsp freshly ground black pepper

PREPARE IT

Heat the oven to 220°C. In a large bowl, combine all the ingredients and knead the dough to a firm consistency. Cover with a tea towel and leave to rest in the fridge for an hour, then turn out onto a clean work surface. Break off walnut-size pieces and roll each piece out as thinly as possible, dusting with flour as you go. The crackers should end up as paper-thin long ovals. Arrange on a paper-lined baking tray. Brush generously with olive oil and bake for 6 minutes until crisp and golden.

Makes 25

Breakfast chef Daniel delights our guests with this mouth-watering Green Shakshuka before their morning safari.

CHILLED BEETROOT SOUP

SHOP IT

6–8 medium-sized beetroots, thoroughly washed

2 cups cold water

2 cups vegetable stock

1 Tbsp sugar

300ml buttermilk

200ml yoghurt plus an extra 50ml for serving

1 Tbsp lemon juice

salt and freshly ground black pepper

fresh dill, finely chopped

PREPARE IT

Peel the beetroot then roughly grate (wear gloves!). Put the beetroot into a large saucepan and cover with water (use more if necessary – it must be covered). Bring to a boil slowly, then turn down the heat and leave to simmer very gently for 20 minutes (they must not boil too rapidly). Once the beetroot has softened, add the stock and sugar. Stir well and refrigerate until completely cold (for at least 4 hours).

Before serving, liquidise the soup and add buttermilk, yoghurt and lemon juice. Season well. Serve with a swirl of yoghurt and dill.

Serves 6

KITCHEN NOTES

At Angama Mara we make all our soups with our own vegetable stock (but a good store-bought one in liquid form works well). This recipe can be prepared with a good chicken stock too.

Ignatius, shamba-keeper and accomplished garden tour leader, has no fight with the elephants. 'They were here first,' he smiles.

ROASTED ROOT VEGETABLE SALAD WITH HONEY DRESSING

SHOP IT

400g carrots, thickly julienned

400g beetroot, thickly julienned

⅓ cup olive oil

½ cup soft brown sugar

salt and freshly ground black pepper

100g fresh rocket (arugula) for serving

Dressing:

¼ cup olive oil

2 Tbsp red wine vinegar

2 Tbsp honey

5 fresh mint leaves, finely chopped

1 tsp ground cumin

1 tsp ground paprika

1 Tbsp Dijon mustard

PREPARE IT

Turn the grill onto its highest setting.

To make the dressing, combine all the ingredients and blend well, using a whisk. Check the seasoning, adding more mustard and honey according to your preference.

Toss the carrot and beetroot sticks (separately) in olive oil and brown sugar, then season well. Roast the vegetables under the grill until tender, taking care not to burn them, but they should have a lovely caramel coating. Allow to cool. Just before serving, mix the rocket and roasted vegetables together and toss generously in the dressing.

Serves 6 as a side salad

Salad queen Brenda starts each day with a visit to the shamba to harvest mustard cress, rocket, red oak leaf lettuce and fennel, among others, for the lunch dishes.

PINEAPPLE & CHILLI ICE CREAM

SHOP IT

2 pineapples, peeled, chopped
and puréed

2 red chillies, seeds removed and
finely julienned

2 Tbsp finely julienned red peppers

300g castor sugar

1 cup water

2 Tbsp lemon juice

6 egg yolks

2 cups fresh cream

pineapple wedges for serving

castor sugar for tossing

butter for browning

PREPARE IT

Place the pineapple purée in a pot and bring to a gentle simmer, allowing it to reduce by half.

Place the julienned chillies and red peppers in a pot with the castor sugar and water. Bring to a boil and cook until syrupy. Set aside some of the chillies for decorating.

Mix the lemon juice, pineapple purée and egg yolks in a heatproof bowl and place over a pot of simmering water. Whisk until the mixture starts to thicken very slightly. Stir in the cream, then leave to cool and churn until set.

Serve the ice cream in scoops decorated with a couple of pieces of chilli from the syrup and wedges of pineapple that have been tossed in castor sugar and browned in butter in a pan.

Serves 6

Samuel and James grow some of the most wicked chillies in the shamba, ideal for Kenya's famous Pili Pili Sauce, which we serve at our barbecue.

FRUIT CARPACCIO
WITH MINT LIME SUGAR & WATERMELON SORBET

At the lodge, the only desserts we serve at lunchtime are homemade ice creams and dishes made with fresh fruits – perfect endings for a safari lunch.

FRUIT CARPACCIO

SHOP IT
a generous handful of fresh mint, roughly chopped

3 Tbsp castor sugar

2 limes, zested and juiced

1 pineapple, peeled and sliced as thinly as possible

1 mango, peeled, pitted and finely diced

6 passionfruit, pulp scooped out

fresh baby basil

PREPARE IT
To make mint-sugar, place the mint in a mortar with the castor sugar and grind down until the sugar turns green. Mix in the lime zest and juice.

Fan the pineapple slices on a plate, top with the mango and passionfruit pulp and generously sprinkle with the mint-sugar and scatter with basil leaves. Serve with a scoop or two of Watermelon Sorbet.

Serves 6

WATERMELON SORBET

SHOP IT
5 cups seedless watermelon chunks

3 limes, juiced

4 sprigs fresh mint

1 cup sugar

PREPARE IT
Blend the watermelon chunks with half the lime juice until smooth, then set aside.

In a small saucepan, combine the mint, sugar and remaining lime juice. Bring to a boil over a medium heat. Reduce the heat and leave to simmer for 5 minutes, stirring occasionally. Allow to cool. Strain the minted syrup into the watermelon purée. Churn the sorbet in an ice cream machine until set.

A TOUCH OF THE MEDITERRANEAN

The sea around the middle

Is it possible for our chefs not to be inspired by the great cooking traditions of the Mediterranean? As a lodge in Africa, we prepare dishes from both the African coastal countries of the Med and those further north, Italy in particular. What comes to mind when we think of Mediterranean food? Olive oil first and foremost, closely followed by tomatoes, ripened on the vine, and not forgetting pasta, pulses, fish, capers and basil.

Every evening, our dinner menu includes a pasta dish and you would be surprised how many of our guests choose it. A complaint we often hear is, 'Too much food – we sit in the safari vehicle for most of the day and for the rest of the time, you feed us.' A wonderful problem to have, we reckon.

Our Moroccan Minestrone straddles both the north and south of the Mediterranean and the Rigatoni with Roasted Tomatoes & Ricotta Salata is a quick fix for a delicious meal. Many of our ingredients for these dishes are grown in our shamba and, although we don't pickle our own capers as yet, the baby leaves of nasturtiums and their flowers grace many of our salads.

MOROCCAN MINESTRONE

SHOP IT

2 tsp olive oil

1 onion, finely chopped

1 tsp grated ginger

1 Tbsp ground cumin

1 Tbsp ground paprika

1 Tbsp ground coriander

3 carrots, finely chopped

2 celery stalks, finely chopped

3 courgettes, finely chopped

1 eggplant, finely chopped

corn cut from 2 corn cobs

4 cups vegetable stock

1 bay leaf

1 x 400g can chopped tomatoes

1 x 400g can chickpeas

¼ cup orzo

fresh coriander and parsley, finely chopped for serving

parmesan cheese, finely grated, for sprinkling

crusty bread

PREPARE IT

Heat the olive oil in a pot and cook the onion until very soft, taking care not to burn it.

Stir in the ginger and ground spices. Add all the remaining vegetables and sauté for 5 minutes. Add the stock, bay leaf, chopped tomatoes and chickpeas. Simmer for 20 minutes.

Just before serving add the orzo and cook until al dente. Scatter over some fresh coriander and parsley and a sprinkling of parmesan cheese. Serve with a crusty bread of your choice.

Serves 4–6

RIGATONI WITH ROASTED TOMATOES & RICOTTA SALATA

Every guest asks us where we source our delicious cheeses, including the ricotta in this recipe. The answer is simple: Browns Cheese in the Limuru Highlands outside of Nairobi. Halloumi, mature cheddar, cream cheese, goat's milk cheese, sheep's milk cheese, camembert and even burrata are all made right here on our doorstep. Well almost.

SHOP IT

1.5kg tomatoes

salt and pepper to taste

4 cloves garlic, unpeeled

5 sprigs fresh thyme

3 bay leaves

a splash of red wine vinegar

500g rigatoni

extra virgin olive oil

100g ricotta, grated

*a small bunch of fresh basil, leaves
    picked for serving*

parmesan, freshly grated for serving

PREPARE IT

Preheat the oven to 200°C.

Arrange the tomatoes on a large baking tray, and season with salt and pepper. Scatter over the garlic cloves, thyme sprigs and bay leaves, then roast for 25 minutes until the tomato skins have blackened and split. Leave the tomatoes to cool, then remove the skins.

Place the peeled tomatoes in a frying pan with the red wine vinegar and a pinch more salt and pepper. Squash with a spoon and allow to simmer for 15 minutes, until it becomes a thick, strawberry-red sauce with an almost creamy-like consistency.

Bring a pan of salted water to a boil and cook the rigatoni according to the packet instructions. Drain, reserving a cupful of cooking water, and add the pasta to the tomato sauce with a little of the cooking water to loosen. Divide the dressed pasta into 4 serving bowls, drizzle generously with the olive oil and top with the grated ricotta and a scattering of basil leaves. Serve with grated parmesan on the side.

Serves 4

NORTH AFRICAN BUTTER BEAN, BARLEY, SWEET POTATO & BUTTERNUT CASSEROLE

Do you remember the days when vegetarians were few and far between? Well, that has changed dramatically, and we would hazard a guess that every single one of our guests enjoys protein-free dishes, even if they are still omnivorously inclined. Vegetarian dishes constitute a third of what we offer our guests at each meal. And vegan and gluten-free don't faze us a bit. If you lose the yoghurt when serving this hearty casserole, it will be vegan all the way. It would also do well as a filling for rotis.

SHOP IT

½ cup olive oil

2 leeks, diced

a bunch of fresh coriander, leaves and stems separated

1 cup finely chopped fresh fennel (reserve a few fronds)

3 cloves garlic, finely chopped

2 ½ Tbsp baharat* *spice mix*

½ stick cinnamon

2 Tbsp tomato paste

2 litres vegetable stock

½ cup pearl barley

salt to taste

a large pinch of saffron

4 cups cooked or canned chickpeas

4 cups cooked or canned butter beans

¾ cup diced sweet potato

2 cups peeled and diced butternut

½ cup red lentils

plain yoghurt for serving

extra-virgin olive oil for drizzling

paprika for sprinkling

PREPARE IT

Heat the oil in a large pot and gently cook the leeks for 10–12 minutes. Finely chop the coriander stems, then add to the leeks along with the fennel and garlic. Cook for 2 minutes. Add the *baharat*, cinnamon and tomato paste and cook for another 2 minutes. Add the stock and barley and season with salt, then bring to a boil. Stir in the saffron and simmer for 40 minutes (adding more water if necessary). Finally, add chickpeas, butter beans, sweet potato, butternut and lentils. Cook until the barley is tender (20–30 minutes). Adjust the seasoning and remove the cinnamon stick.

To serve, ladle into bowls and top with some yoghurt or serve on the side. Drizzle with olive oil, garnish with the coriander leaves and reserved fennel fronds, then sprinkle with paprika.

Serves 8

KITCHEN NOTE*

To make *baharat*, combine 2 Tbsp paprika, 1 Tbsp ground coriander, 1 Tbsp ground cumin, 1 Tbsp ground turmeric, 2 tsp freshly ground black pepper, 1 tsp grated nutmeg, 1 tsp ground cardamom and 1 tsp allspice. Seal in an airtight container.

RICOTTA PANCAKES WITH CARDAMOM SUGAR, MAASAI HONEY & FRIED BANANAS

Strictly speaking, bananas are not very Mediterranean, but fried they marry so well with honey and ricotta. So we indulged in a little poetic licence. Speaking of bananas , they are a staple diet across Kenya. The ones we love best are the lady finger bananas, also known as sugar bananas. Keep an eye out for them; they taste as delicious as their name sounds.

SHOP IT

1 Tbsp freshly ground cardamom

½ cup castor sugar

1 cup cake flour

1 Tbsp baking powder

a good pinch of salt

3 Tbsp castor sugar

2 Tbsp vegetable oil

2 eggs, separated

1 cup milk, or as needed

*½ cup ricotta, softened with milk
   or yoghurt*

100g butter, plus extra for serving

6 bananas (or 12 lady finger bananas)

*Maasai honey (or a strong dark honey)
   for serving*

PREPARE IT

Combine the cardamom and half a cup of castor sugar, then set aside. Sift together the flour, baking powder, salt and 3 tablespoons of castor sugar. Whisk together the oil, egg yolks, milk and ricotta or yoghurt. Make a well in the dry ingredients and pour in egg mixture. Gently fold together, adding more milk if necessary and taking care not to overmix as the batter will become too heavy. Refrigerate for 30 minutes.

Beat the egg whites until stiff, and gently fold into the batter. Heat the butter in a frying pan and sauté the bananas until cooked and golden. Set aside.

Heat a heavy-based frying pan and add a little oil. Drop a large spoonful of batter into the pan and cook on one side until bubbles start to appear on the surface. Gently flip the pancake over and cook on the other side until just done. Repeat with the remaining batter.

To serve, place a knob of butter between two pancakes, sprinkle with cardamom-sugar and serve with fried bananas and honey on the side.

Serves 6

KITCHEN NOTE

It goes without saying that these pancakes are delicious served with crispy bacon.

Chef Moses is surely one of the best pancake-flippers in all of Kenya.

ON THE *OUT OF AFRICA* KOPJE

I had a farm in Africa

About forty years ago, location scouts for the upcoming filming of Karen Blixen's great African memoir *Out of Africa* stumbled across a remote corner of the Mara Triangle that would easily pass for the famous Ngong Hills in Blixen's opening sentence. This is where we built Angama Mara. And that is what inspired the title of this book.

The kopje, or small hill, featured on the movie's poster with Meryl Streep and Robert Redford in the foreground, is where our guests enjoy romantic picnics. The views are heart-stopping and the sparkling wine well chilled. Perched on the edge of the Rift Valley, this private hideaway is fast becoming *the* place to propose and so far, every answer has been YES.

Our butlers don their handsome white kanga tops and lay out a picnic featuring lovely colonial-era paraphernalia, right down to checked or striped blankets. This is the only corner of the guest experience where we indulge in a little colonial-style safari chic.

Scattered throughout the lodge and the property are many other touch points from the movie and every tent has a copy of *Out of Africa*, waiting to be read. Guests often settle in our library to watch the movie, with the fire blazing, red wine flowing, a bowl of Spiced Popcorn and a ready supply of tissues.

MAASAI HONEY BISCUITS

It feels as though every tree in Maasailand has a traditional honey hive hanging from it; and how delighted we are to have dark, smoky, organic, delicious honey on tap all year round. Many of the surrounding homesteads have hives suspended from strung wire around their own shambas. When the elephants come visiting, the instant they hit the wire the bees start alarming and that's enough to send Africa's greatest land mammals scurrying for their lives.

SHOP IT

125g butter

½ cup sugar

*1 Tbsp Maasai honey
(or a dark smoky honey)*

1 Tbsp milk

1 ½ cups cake flour, sifted

1 tsp baking powder

PREPARE IT

Preheat the oven to 180°C.

In a pot, combine the butter, sugar, milk and honey over heat, stirring constantly until almost boiling. Allow to cool.

Once the liquid is lukewarm, stir in the flour and baking powder. Roll about 1 tablespoon of dough into a ball and press flat. Repeat with the remaining dough and arrange the biscuits on a baking tray. Bake for 15 minutes until golden. Leave to cool on a wire rack.

Makes 30

CHEESY BRIOCHE ROLLS

These delicious Cheesy Brioche Rolls were brought to our kitchen by Chef Graeme from the UK. Graeme and I go back to when we opened The Bay Hotel in Cape Town in 1989. He is a remarkable chef if not a little scary to us bush types, but we so enjoyed having him train our team.

SHOP IT
¾ cup flour

4 tsp dried yeast

½ cup lukewarm water

4 cups flour

3 tsp salt

3 Tbsp sugar

8 large eggs

500g butter, melted but not separated

300g strong cheddar, grated

PREPARE IT

Mix together the three-quarter cup of flour, yeast and lukewarm water, and leave to rise for 3 hours.

When ready, place the dough in a mixer fitted with a dough hook and set to a medium speed. Add the 4 cups of flour, salt and sugar. Mix for 5 minutes, then increase the mixer setting up one notch and add the eggs, one by one. Pour in the melted butter and, once mixed in, add the grated cheese. Cover the dough and refrigerate for a minimum of 6 hours or a maximum of 4 days.

Preheat the oven to 220°C and oil three muffin trays, each with a capacity of 12 cups. Portion the dough into golf ball-sized balls, place in the prepared muffin trays, cover and leave to prove until doubled in size. Bake for 20 minutes (turning halfway) until golden and crispy.

Makes 36 rolls

LIFE-CHANGING SEED BREAD

If this recipe is life changing, so was the day Amanda joined our kitchen family as our principle chef trainer. Amanda spends two weeks twice a year with us and brings joy, calm, creativity and consistency to the team. We simply could not survive without her. Oh, and every food image in this book was prepared by her and the Angama team.

SHOP IT

1 cup sunflower seeds

½ cup flax seeds (linseeds)

½ cup chopped almonds

1 ½ cups rolled oats

2 Tbsp chia seeds

4 Tbsp psyllium seed husks or 3 Tbsp psyllium husk powder)

1 tsp salt

1 tsp syrup or honey

3 Tbsp coconut oil or melted butter

1 ½ cups water

PREPARE IT

Combine all the seeds, nuts, oats, psyllium husks and salt until well mixed.

Whisk together the syrup or honey, coconut oil or melted butter, and water. Add this to the dry ingredients and mix until everything is completely soaked and the dough becomes very thick. Place in an oiled loaf pan and leave out for 2 hours at least, or all day or overnight.

Preheat the oven to 180°C. Bake the loaf for 20 minutes, then turn out, upside-down, onto an oven rack and bake for another 30–40 minutes. Allow to cool completely before slicing.

Makes 1 loaf

KITCHEN NOTE
This bread freezes well.

WATERMELON SKEWERS
WITH LEMON SYRUP & MINT SUGAR

SHOP IT

1 ½ cups castor sugar

¾ cup water

1 lemon, juiced and rind julienned

½ cup castor sugar

½ cup finely chopped mint

10 skewers

*1 small watermelon, peeled,
    cut into 3cm cubes or wedges
    and pips removed*

purple basil or mint for decorating

PREPARE IT

Add one-and-a-half cups of the sugar to a small pot, along with the water and julienned lemon rind. Bring to a boil then allow to reduce to 1 cup of syrup and stir in the lemon juice. Leave to cool.

Mix the remaining castor sugar and mint together in a mortar until the sugar turns green, then set aside.

Thread 5 cubes of watermelon onto each skewer, arrange on a plate and generously drizzle with the lemon syrup. Just before serving, generously sprinkle with the mint sugar.

Serve chilled and decorated with purple basil or mint.

Serves 10

A kitchen team in the middle of nowhere is only as good as its back-up in supplies. Mike, our storekeeper-in-chief, ensures that we never run out of anything, and that we always receive the freshest produce at the best prices.

PICNICS ON SAFARI

It wouldn't be a picnic without the elephants

Our very best safari day at Angama Mara is a double picnic day: early wake-up to watch the hot air balloons float by as the sun breaks the horizon, down a good cappuccino and a Maasai Honey Biscuit, grab your camera and binos and set off into the Reserve.

Our guides have food a-plenty packed in the safari vehicle for a full day's adventure, which will take you all the way down to the border with Tanzania (for that shot with your feet in two countries). First stop is a picnic breakfast under a towering fig tree without another soul in sight, but maybe an elephant or two for company, which of course is preferable to a family of meal-seeking lions. A few hours later, it's time for a picnic lunch either by the Mara River with crocs and hippo for company or under another lone tree out on the savanna. Chilled rosé wine, ice-cold Tuskers (Kenya's iconic beer) or maybe a G&T, all at the ready. And then slowly head back to camp – a perfect day.

None of the above would be possible without the early-rising, dedicated team of chefs. First up is the baker because the rolls have to be fresh. Next to arrive are the picnic chefs because all the dishes have to be prepared on the day. On busy days they can prepare up to 60 picnics, with the first guest departures at 5.45am. All the picnics are packed individually (only in sustainable containers), according to our guests' dietary needs. And, of course, children are treated to extra Salted Caramel Brownies in their picnic tins.

PASSIONFRUIT & GINGER ICED TEA , MANGO LASSI & PINK LEMONADE

PASSIONFRUIT & GINGER ICED TEA

SHOP IT
1 litre water

1/2 cup sugar

5 thick fingers fresh ginger, peeled

6 green tea bags

2 cups passionfruit pulp

PREPARE IT
Combine the water, sugar and ginger in a saucepan and bring to a boil. Simmer for 2 minutes, stirring until the sugar has dissolved. Remove from the heat and add the tea bags. Let them steep for 30 minutes, strain and allow to cool. Once cooled, stir in the passionfruit pulp.

MANGO LASSI

SHOP IT
4 large mangoes, peeled, pitted and cubed

1 cup yoghurt

1 cup orange juice

1 tsp vanilla essence

sugar to taste

PREPARE IT
In a blender, combine all ingredients. Blend until smooth. Serve chilled.

PINK LEMONADE

SHOP IT
1/2 cup sugar

4 limes, rind peeled in ribbons

5 1/2 cups of water

2 cups fresh lime juice

1/4 cup cranberry juice

1/8 tsp salt

PREPARE IT
Combine the sugar, lime rind and half a cup of the water in a saucepan. Bring to a boil and simmer until the sugar has dissolved. Remove from the heat.

In a large jug, combine the remaining water, lime juice, cranberry juice and salt. Discard the lime peels from the syrup and add to the lemonade. Stir well. Pour through a fine sieve.

Serve chilled.

Chef Jackson prepares all the fresh juices, smoothies and lemonades served at the lodge with love. 'My guests like to stay healthy and strong' is his favourite comment.

UGANDAN ROLEX

Rolex from Uganda? Yes indeed. The very best for that matter. This much-loved street dish is simply a flavoured omelette wrapped in a chapatti. Rolled eggs. Get it?

SHOP IT

1 tsp harissa paste

1 Tbsp yoghurt

a squeeze of lemon juice

salt to taste

½ tsp ground cumin

1 chapatti, roti or tortilla

2 eggs

3 spring onions, finely chopped

½ red pepper, finely cubed

¼ red chilli, seeds removed and finely sliced

1 tsp chives, snipped

2 Tbsp grated strong cheddar cheese

2 Tbsp butter

PREPARE IT

Mix the harissa paste with the yoghurt, then season with the lemon juice, salt and ground cumin to taste.

Warm the chapatti, roti or tortilla in a hot, dry frying pan. Spread with the harissa mix.

In a bowl, lightly beat the eggs and add the spring onions, red pepper, chilli, chives, cheddar cheese and salt to taste. Melt the butter in an omelette pan, add the egg mixture and cook until firm.

Place the cooked omelette on the chapatti and roll up tightly.

Serves 1

A star member of the Angama Football Club (affectionately known as AFC whose home ground goes by the name of the Slaughter House), Chef Hudson is also our picnic maestro and whatever you do, don't borrow his favourite knife.

PICKLED FISH WITH LEMON & CORIANDER

The opening chapter of my food story was set in the early 1980s at The Arniston Hotel, a little beach hotel near the southernmost point of Africa. Here I learnt from Trienie and Poppie, my beloved chefs, how to make Pickled Fish. This dish has travelled with me through Africa, finally finding its home in the Mara.

SHOP IT

2 tsp olive oil

2 large onions, halved and thinly sliced

2 Tbsp garlic, finely chopped

2 tsp ginger, finely grated

4 tsp mild curry powder

4 tsp turmeric

2 tsp ground cumin

2 tsp ground coriander

2 tsp yellow mustard seeds

2 Tbsp sugar

½ tsp salt

2 bay leaves

½ cup white wine vinegar

1½ cups fish or vegetable stock

700g fresh firm-fleshed fish
    fillets, cubed

¼ cup cake flour

salt and freshly ground black pepper
    to taste

½ cup sunflower oil

lemon cheeks and fresh coriander
    leaves for serving

PREPARE IT

Heat the olive oil in a heavy-based saucepan over a medium heat. Add the onions and sauté for 5 minutes. Stir in the the garlic, ginger, curry powder, turmeric, cumin, coriander, mustard seeds, sugar and salt. Fry for 2 minutes, then add the bay leaves, vinegar and stock. Bring to a boil and cook for 5 minutes until the mixture thickens and becomes syrupy.

Season the flour with salt and pepper and use to coat the fish. Shallow fry the fish in a large frying pan in the sunflower oil. Pack the fish in a glass bowl, and pour over the curried sauce. Leave for 24 hours or longer before serving.

Serve cold, scattered with fresh coriander leaves and cheeks of lemon.

Serves 4

SALTED CARAMEL BROWNIES

We are smitten by Deb Perlman's blog 'Smitten Kitchen' and these salty, caramelly brownies are inspired by her recipe. After all what could be a better combo than flaked salt, dark chocolate and perfectly cooked caramel?

SHOP IT

1 ¹/₃ cup butter

3 cups white sugar

4 eggs

2 tsp vanilla essence

1 ¹/₂ cups cake flour

¹/₂ tsp salt

1 cup cocoa powder

Salted caramel:

¹/₂ cup light brown sugar

3 Tbsp salted butter

4 Tbsp fresh cream

¹/₄ tsp salt

PREPARE IT

First make the salted caramel. Line a baking sheet with a square of lightly buttered parchment paper. In a medium-sized, heavy-bottomed saucepan, over a medium-high heat, melt the brown sugar until it turns a dark golden colour. Remove from the heat and stir in butter, cream and salt and bring back to a simmer, melting any sugar that may have solidified. Cook the bubbling caramel for a few minutes more, until it is a shade darker. Pour out onto the prepared baking sheet to set and then transfer to the freezer.

Preheat the oven to 170°C. Grease and line a 25cm-square baking tin with parchment paper.

Beat the butter and sugar with the eggs until light and fluffy, then add the vanilla essence. Sift together the flour, salt and cocoa powder, then add to the egg mixture and stir well until just blended; do not overbeat. Pour into the prepared baking tin, spreading evenly. Break up the caramel into big chunks and scatter over the mixture. Bake for about 1 hour until the brownies sink and come away a little from the sides of the pan. Prick with a toothpick: if crumbs stick to the toothpick, the brownies are done. Cool in the tin on a wire rack then cut into squares or triangles.

Makes 16–25 squares (depending on size)

It's up at 1am for Chef Kina and, despite the hour, she always looks this happy. Kina is our rocket-powered bread baker, dessert chef and ice cream magician.

FROM SOMEWHERE IN THE MIDDLE EAST

Ode to Chef O

In his first interview for head chef position, Chef Collins was shown *Ottolenghi: The Cookbook* and was informed 'This is what our Angama food will be'. He flipped through the pages nonchalantly, saying it looked easy, really quite do-able. He was then asked to read the recipes. And the colour drained from his face as he took in the staggering number of exotic ingredients (well, by Kenyan standards, anyway). Then he read the methods a little more closely and started to panic with all the chopping and preparation that goes into Ottolenghi's recipes.

But that was all then, way back in early 2015. Now Yottam Ottolenghi, or Chef O, as he is affectionately known in our kitchen, is part of the team, with his books all sauce-splattered and dog-eared. Our Maasai chefs, many of whom have as yet to visit Nairobi, let alone travel abroad, finish their dishes with sumac, za'atar and black sesame seeds as if they were sprigs of parsley. How far we have all come, out here in the Mara. And, even though he doesn't know it, much credit goes to Chef O. What a grand day it would be when he comes to stay at our lodge.

MIDDLE EASTERN BREAKFAST

The overriding food memory of our guests is probably the quantity of chapattis they devoured during their safari. Making chapattis is a fine art and one to be avoided if someone else can make them better. They feature on our breakfast, picnic, lunch, dinner and barbecue menus. Chapattis every which way. This dish was discovered at a small all-day breakfast joint in Jo'burg, Pablo Eggs-Go-Bar. The name cracks us up.

SHOP IT

1 chapatti, roti or tortilla

3 Tbsp hummus

paprika and za'atar for garnishing

2 eggs, hard boiled, peeled and sliced

3 Tbsp finely diced tomato, onion and cucumber (salsa)

olive oil

fresh parsley, chopped

1 Tbsp pine nuts, toasted

PREPARE IT

Place a warm chapatti, roti or tortilla on a dinner plate and top with a layer of hummus sprinkled with paprika. Place sliced hard-boiled eggs down one half and the tomato salsa down the other. Sprinkle za'atar over the eggs. Drizzle with olive oil and finally scatter with chopped parsley and the pine nuts.

Serves 1

HUMMUS TOASTIE WITH POACHED EGG, AVO, FETA, TOMATOES, ROCKET & ZA'ATAR

At Angama, the chefs make hummus by the 5-litre bucket. How many people do you know who sneak into the fridge at all hours of the day and night to scoop with their finger a huge dollop of this soul food? Heaps. And we are as addicted as the rest. Hummus on the breakfast menu. Tick. Hummus on our lunch menu. Done. Hummus at the barbecue. Always.

SHOP IT

2 slices sourdough bread

2 Tbsp butter

2 eggs

butter for frying

4 Tbsp hummus

a small handful of fresh rocket (arugula)

½ avocado, peeled and sliced

1 tomato, sliced

2 Tbsp crumbled feta

za'atar and alfalfa sprouts for garnishing

PREPARE IT

Spread both sides of the sourdough with the butter and pan-fry until crisp and golden.

Poach or fry the eggs in butter, according to taste.

On a dinner plate assemble as follows: the toasted bread spread with hummus, then topped with rocket, avocado, tomato, feta and, finally, an egg. Sprinkle generously with za'atar and scatter with alfalfa sprouts.

Serves 1

'Easy peasy' is the favourite phrase of Maasai Mzee and unflappable Senior Chef Joseph.

DUKKA & ROSEMARY FOCACCIA

DUKKA

SHOP IT

1 cup macadamia nuts

1 cup hazelnuts

1 cup cashew nuts or skinned raw peanuts

1 cup pistachio nuts

½ cup pumpkin seeds

½ cup sesame seeds

½ cup sunflower seeds

2 Tbsp ground cumin

1 Tbsp ground cinnamon

½ tsp ground cloves

1 Tbsp salt

1 Tbsp freshly ground black pepper

PREPARE IT

Preheat the oven to 180°C. Spread the nuts on an oven tray (40 x 60cm), then place the seeds on another, separate tray. Roast the nuts and toast the seeds in the oven until all are golden-brown. The pumpkin seeds and sesame seeds will start to pop and jump when they are ready.

Place the nuts, cumin, cinnamon, cloves, salt and pepper in a food processor and pulse until most – but not all – the nuts are broken up. Mix in the seeds. Transfer the dukka to an airtight container.

Makes 5 cups

ROSEMARY FOCACCIA

SHOP IT

1kg flour

30g dried yeast

2 cups warm water

4 Tbsp olive oil

2 tsp salt

½ cup pitted black olives

Rosemary sprigs

PREPARE IT

Preheat the oven to 220°C.

Place all the ingredients, except the rosemary, in a mixer and blend with a dough hook until it comes together. Leave the dough to rest for 10 minutes in the bowl, then transfer to an oiled baking tray. Rub the dough with a little more oil. Leave for a further 10 minutes, then roll out very gently from the centre, first upwards then downwards, once each. Leave for 20 minutes until doubled in size. Use the tip of a wooden spoon to make dimples in the dough. Tuck a sprig of rosemary and one olive in each dimple. Bake for 20–25 minutes until golden-brown in colour.

Makes 1 tray (40 x 60cm)

CUMIN-SPICED LAMB KOFTAS WITH SMOKY EGGPLANT

CUMIN-SPICED LAMB KOFTAS

SHOP IT

1 Tbsp ground cumin

2 tsp ground coriander

1 tsp turmeric

500g lamb mince

1 red onion, finely chopped

3 cloves garlic, peeled and crushed

1 lemon, juiced and zested

salt and pepper to taste

2 Tbsp each chopped fresh mint, parsley and coriander

1 egg

12 skewers

200ml yoghurt

4 Tbsp tahini

vegetable oil for frying

4 tomatoes, sliced and seasoned

1 red chilli, thinly sliced for garnishing

PREPARE IT

Fry the cumin, coriander and turmeric in a dry pan, lightly toasting the spices. Place the spices, lamb mince, onion, garlic, lemon juice and zest, salt and pepper, chopped herbs and egg in a bowl and mix thoroughly until well combined. Form the mixture into oval-shaped meatballs (koftas) onto the end of each skewer and refrigerate for 15 minutes.

Meanwhile, mix the yoghurt and tahini and set aside.

Gently fry the koftas in a little oil, until well browned and cooked through. Serve on tomato and onion slices, topped with tahini-yoghurt sauce and sprinkle with chopped coriander and slices of chilli. Place a dish of the Smoky Eggplant on the side.

Serves 4

SMOKY EGGPLANT

SHOP IT

2 Tbsp olive oil

1 tsp salt

2 medium eggplants, well pricked with a fork

6 Tbsp tahini

2 cloves garlic, peeled and crushed

juice of 1 lemon

a pinch of cayenne pepper

1–2 pinches of ground cumin

2 Tbsp chopped fresh parsley

toasted sesame seeds and za'atar for garnishing

PREPARE IT

Preheat the oven to 180°C. Brush a baking sheet with half of the olive oil and sprinkle with the salt. Over a gas flame, evenly char the skin of the eggplants. When cool enough to handle, trim off the stem and halve lengthways. Place cut sides down on the baking sheet and roast for 30–35 minutes, until very tender when pressed. Cool to room temperature then scrape out the flesh and place in a blender with the tahini, garlic, lemon juice, cayenne pepper, cumin and half the parsley. Pulse until combined but still coarse. Check for seasoning. Spoon into a bowl, drizzle with the remaining olive oil and scatter with the rest of the parsley, sesame seeds and za'atar. Refrigerate until needed, but serve at room temperature.

TOASTED ALMOND & CARDAMOM ICE CREAM WITH ALMOND BISCOTTI

There is a legend that, once upon a time, a Moorish king in today's modern Spain planted thousands of almond trees for his Scandinavian-born love who missed her snowy homeland. Remember this romantic tale next time you cook with almonds and there is sure to be love in that dish.

TOASTED ALMOND & CARDAMOM ICE CREAM

SHOP IT

100g butter

15 cardamom pods, crushed

½ tsp ground cinnamon

50g castor sugar

1 cup milk

1 cup fresh cream

1 tsp vanilla essence

6 egg yolks

50g slivered almonds

PREPARE IT

Melt the butter in a saucepan. Add the crushed cardamom, cinnamon and sugar. Pour in the milk and cream and bring to a boil. Remove from the heat and allow to stand for 15 minutes. Stir in the vanilla essence.

Place the egg yolks in a bowl and slowly whisk in the milk mixture. Pour the mixture back into the saucepan and gently simmer until it coats the back of a spoon. Do not boil or the mixture will curdle. Remove from the heat and refrigerate to chill, stirring every so often. Once chilled, strain and churn in an ice-cream maker.

Roast the almonds in a dry pan until golden-brown and allow to cool. Stir the almonds into the churned ice-cream mixture. Freeze until serving.

Serves 6

ALMOND BISCOTTI

SHOP IT

8 egg whites

240g sugar

2 Tbsp vanilla essence

240g cake flour, sifted

240g whole almonds, skin on

PREPARE IT

Preheat the oven to 180°C. Grease a loaf tin.

Beat the egg whites, sugar and vanilla essence, then fold in the flour and almonds. Spoon into the prepared loaf tin and bake for 45 minutes. Turn out the loaf and leave to cool on a wire rack. Once cold, wrap in plastic wrap and freeze for 12 hours. Thinly slice as much of the biscotti as you need, place on a baking sheet and bake at 130°C for 30 minutes or until dry. Store in an airtight container. Keep the rest of the biscotti loaf in the freezer until required again.

IN THE MAASAI BOMA

Happiness is as good as food – Maasai proverb

When in Maasailand, toasting the sunset is our interpretation of the above. Most evenings our guests gather in our Maasai boma, which has sweeping views of the Mara almost all the way down to Tanzania, the *Out of Africa* kopje, and the Oloololo Escarpment, a marvellous word in Ma meaning zigzag. Here they share stories of the day, down dawas at an alarming rate, feast on bitings cooked on the coals and try their hand at jumping and singing with the warriors as they perform their traditional, haunting dances around a blazing fire bowl.

The drink hero of the evening is the infamous and somewhat lethal Kenyan Dawa. Those who know only too well the effects of too many back-to-back mojitos will sympathise. 'Dawa' translated from Swahili to English means 'medicine'. Take that as you please. Another Kenyan favourite served in our boma are Karanga Nuts. Make double the quantity because, for some strange reason, they seem to evaporate.

KENYAN DAWA & CHARGRILLED TOMATO BREAD

KENYAN DAWA

SHOP IT

1 lime, quartered

honey

6 ice cubes

2 tots vodka

PREPARE IT

Place the lime quarters in a glass. Twirl the dawa stick* into the honey pot, place the stick in the glass and gently bash the limes. Add 6 ice cubes and pour 2 tots of vodka over the ice. Bash a little more to mix in the vodka.

Serves 1

KITCHEN NOTE*

Dawa sticks can be made by cutting a 1.5cm round wooden dowel stick into 15cm lengths.

CHARGRILLED TOMATO BREAD

SHOP IT

4 slices ciabatta or sourdough bread

olive oil for brushing and dressing

1 garlic clove, halved

4 tomatoes, grated

salt and freshly ground black pepper to taste

PREPARE IT

Preheat the grill.

Brush the bread with olive oil and toast well under the grill. Rub the hot bread with garlic and top with the grated tomato (discarding the garlic). Season with salt and pepper and serve with a final swirl of good olive oil.

Serves 4

Adam, our inhouse photographer, is also the photography studio host, private wildlife photographic guide and, when sweetly asked, people photographer. He captured most of the images of the Angama family for this book. Oh, and he is also a 'lion-ophile'.

SPICY POPCORN
& KARANGA NUTS

What is it about popcorn straight out of the pot that is so irresistible? We watch in amazement as our well-travelled, fine-palated and discerning guests grab a whole bowlful of Spiced Popcorn or Karanga Nuts and flatten it. 'Karanga' is the Swahili word for nuts.

KARANGA NUTS

SHOP IT
1 cup raw cashew nuts

1 cup raw almonds, skin on

1 cup raw macadamia nuts

vegetable oil

¼ cup sesame seeds

¼ cup sunflower seeds

¼ cup pumpkin seeds

1 Tbsp fennel seeds

1 cup light brown sugar

2 Tbsp ground masala spice

1 tsp salt

PREPARE IT
In a large frying pan, roast the nuts separately in very little oil, until golden (stir continuously to prevent them from burning.) Drain on kitchen paper and mix the nuts. Dry-toast the seeds separately. Grease a baking tray with a little oil. Melt the sugar in a heavy-based saucepan over a low heat until a light caramel forms, then stir in the masala and fennel seeds until combined. Add the salt, the other seeds and all the nuts to the sugar and stir quickly. Spread 1cm-thick over a greased baking tray. Work quickly, otherwise the sugar will cool and harden. Once completely cool, break into bite-sized pieces. Store in an airtight container for up to 1 month.

Makes 4 cups

SPICY POPCORN

SHOP IT
1 tsp paprika

1 tsp salt

1 tsp pepper

½ tsp cayenne pepper

1 tsp ground cumin

4 cups warm popped popcorn

PREPARE IT
Mix the spices together and toss over the popcorn, while still warm.

PRAWN POTSTICKERS WITH TERIYAKI SAUCE

This is another one of Training Chef Amanda's delicious snack dishes, or bitings as we call them in these parts. We never make quite enough of these so be sure not to repeat that mistake.

SHOP IT

500g cooked prawn meat

2 Tbsp fish sauce

4 Tbsp finely snipped chives

½ cup chopped fresh coriander

3 Tbsp finely julienned fresh ginger

4 Tbsp sweet chilli sauce

salt and freshly ground pepper to taste

oil for frying

samosa wrappers

Teriyaki sauce:

¼ cup light soy sauce

½ cup fresh orange juice

3 Tbsp honey

1 Tbsp grated fresh ginger

1 tsp grated garlic

1 tsp sesame oil

2 tsp cornflour mixed in a little water for thickening

1 Tbsp finely chopped fresh coriander

1 Tbsp thinly sliced spring onions

PREPARE IT

First make the Teriyaki Sauce. Whisk the soy sauce, orange juice, honey, ginger, garlic and oil together in a small pot over a high heat. When it boils, thicken with the cornflour to make it syrupy. Leave to cool then add the coriander and spring onions before serving.

Chop the prawn meat and place in the bowl of a food processor. Process to a rough paste and add the fish sauce, chives, coriander, ginger and sweet chilli sauce. Mix well and season to taste.

Cut the samosa wrappers into 10cm rounds. Fill the centre of each round with the prawn mixture and fold over using a flour and water paste to seal the edges. Deep-fry in oil until golden and serve with the Teriyaki Sauce on the side. As an option, serve on a bed of fried kale.

Makes 36

KITCHEN NOTE

Samosa wrappers can be bought in your local supermarket or made using homemade pasta dough. The wrappers come frozen in strips about 8cm wide and 24cm long. Fold over and cut in a half moon, getting 2 potstickers from each strip.

COURGETTE & HALLOUMI FRITTERS

SHOP IT

3 courgettes, coarsely grated

1 tsp salt

½ red onion, finely chopped

2 cloves garlic, crushed

2 limes, finely zested

60g self-raising flour

2 eggs, lightly beaten

2 ½ tsp ground coriander

1 ½ tsp ground cardamom

150g halloumi, broken into small chunks

salt and freshly ground black pepper to taste

vegetable oil for frying

Lime & coriander sour cream:

200ml sour cream

1 Tbsp finely chopped fresh coriander

½ tsp ground cardamom

1 lime, juiced and finely zested

salt and freshly ground black pepper to taste

PREPARE IT

Mix together all ingredients for the lime and coriander sour cream, check the seasoning and set aside.

Place the courgettes in a colander and sprinkle them with the salt. Drain for 10 minutes, then squeeze to remove most of the liquid. In a bowl, combine the courgettes, onion, garlic, lime zest, flour, eggs, coriander, cardamom and salt and pepper. Mix well, then fold in the halloumi. Shape into fritters and deep-fry until golden and crisp. Drain on kitchen paper and serve hot with the sour cream.

Serves 8

Chef James is usually found behind the grill, turning out perfect steaks for our guests. Courgettes count among his favourite ingredients, the flowers in particular, which he stuffs with ricotta before dipping into a tempura batter and deep-frying.

MORE THAN A TOUCH OF INDIA

And there came two sisters

We are never shy to ask for input on our food, and guests are often invited by the chefs to teach them new dishes, or improve on our current offerings. If guests request a dish that we have never made, we sweetly ask them to teach us. A bit cheeky if you think how much a safari to Africa costs, but they love it. One Friday, the bakers had a challah lesson in preparation for a shabbat meal.

A chance meeting on a flight, just after we had opened, resulted in a culinary coup for Angama Mara. Shaheen and Faheen, and their darling mother Suli, are regulars in our kitchen and their Indian food is simply sublime. The quantities of garlic, fresh ginger and chillies prepared for their food workshops is staggering. And we especially love the way the sisters argue about what spice goes into which dish and who is the better cook. In this chapter, five recipes are dedicated to our Indian sisters, and Suli too, of course.

Indian food is so interwoven into everyday Kenyan food, starting and probably ending with chapattis, that you would be forgiven if sometimes you think you are in India. Spices fresh in from the coast, every chilli on the Scoville scale, puris, parathas, rotis and pulses of every shape and hue abound in the markets across Kenya. And on our menus, naturally.

INDIAN OMELETTE WITH PURIS & GINGER CHAI

These dishes simply cannot be served one without the other two. An Indian trilogy, if you will. And make extra puris (deep-fried bread). They won't go to waste.

INDIAN OMELETTE

SHOP IT
½ *red onion, sliced*

1 small green chilli, seeds removed and chopped

½ *tsp chilli powder*

2 eggs, lightly beaten

salt to taste

1 Tbsp cooking oil

sliced red chilli for garnishing

PREPARE IT
Mix all the ingredients, except the oil, together. Heat the oil in a small frying pan. Pour in the egg mixture and cook one side until nicely browned. Turn and cook the other side. Garnish with the chilli before serving.

Serves 1

PURIS

SHOP IT
½ *cup wholeweat flour*

½ *cup cake flour*

½ *tsp salt*

1 Tbsp cooking oil, plus extra for frying

¼ *cup warm water*

PREPARE IT
Combine the flours and add the salt. Make a well in the centre and pour in the oil. Slowly add warm water, kneading all the time until a stiff dough forms (adjusting the water as necessary: the dough must not be sticky or loose). Divide the dough into small pucks and brush each with oil. Flatten with a rolling pin. In a deep pot, pour in oil to a depth of 1.5cm and heat. Deep-fry the puris, three at a time, pressing them under the oil until brown and puffy. Drain on kitchen paper and serve warm.

Makes 12

GINGER CHAI

SHOP IT
1 ½ *cups milk*

2 ½ *cups water*

3cm peeled fresh ginger, grated

3 tsp sugar

5 teabags, leaves removed and bags discarded

PREPARE IT
Bring the milk and water to a boil in a pot. Add the ginger and sugar. Add the tea leaves and boil for 10 minutes until the tea turns a caramel-brown colour. Strain and serve hot.

Serves 12

The breakfast charge at Angama is bravely led by Chef Loitaba. Once a guest asked him to make scrambled eggs with 22 eggs. He didn't blink.

INDIAN SPICED CAULIFLOWER SOUP

The choice of good Indian restaurants in Nairobi is overwhelming, but our favourite is Open House. Start with Special Ginger Chicken Wings to share and be sure to order double what your instinct tells you. They are that good.

SHOP IT

2 Tbsp olive oil

½ tsp whole cumin seeds

¼ tsp whole fennel seeds

1 medium red onion, chopped

1 medium potato, peeled and chopped

2 tsp fresh ginger, peeled and chopped

2 cloves garlic, peeled and chopped

1 fresh hot green chilli, finely chopped

2 tsp ground coriander

1 tsp ground cumin

¼ tsp ground turmeric

¼ tsp red chilli powder or cayenne pepper to taste

3 ½ cups cauliflower florets

2 medium tomatoes, peeled and chopped

1 ½ tsp salt, or to taste

4 cups water

6 Tbsp plain yoghurt

lime wedges

freshly ground black pepper to taste

½ cup cooked basmati or other long-grain white rice

a handful of fresh coriander, chopped

PREPARE IT

Heat the oil in a large pot over a medium-high heat. Add the cumin seeds and a few seconds later the fennel seeds. After 2 seconds, add the onion and potato. Stir and sauté for 5 minutes. Add the ginger, garlic and green chilli, then fry for 1 minute.

Turn the heat to medium-low and add the ground coriander, cumin, turmeric and chilli powder or cayenne pepper. Stir for 1 minute. Add the cauliflower, tomatoes and salt and cook for 1 minute. Pour in the water, stir and bring to a boil over a medium-high heat. Cover, lower the heat again, and simmer for 25 minutes.

Let the soup cool slightly, then blend half of it and mix with the remaining unblended soup. Adjust the seasoning as needed.

Ladle into bowls and add a dollop of yoghurt. Squeeze lime juice over, add a few grinds of black pepper. Spoon 2 tablespoons of the rice in the centre of each bowl. Scatter with the coriander.

Serves 6

GOAN FISH CURRY
WITH PINEAPPLE CHUTNEY

A flashback to Kenya under British colonial rule is illustrated by the tradition of employing Goan cooks in domestic households and on the ships that sailed from India to East Africa. The great British explorers Burton and Speke took two Goan cooks on their expedition to the Great Lakes of East Africa. Who knew?

GOAN FISH CURRY

SHOP IT

1 onion, finely chopped

2 cloves garlic, finely chopped

1 Tbsp grated fresh ginger

1 tsp turmeric

1 tsp garam masala

1 tsp paprika

1 tsp ground coriander

1 Tbsp tamarind paste

1 Tbsp red curry paste

2 Tbsp medium curry powder

1 tsp chopped red chilli

3 Tbsp tomato paste

500g tomatoes, peeled and roughly chopped

2 tsp brown sugar

salt and freshly ground black pepper to taste

2 cups coconut milk

750g firm white fish fillets

juice of 1 lemon

¼ cup vegetable oil

a bunch of fresh coriander, chopped

PINEAPPLE CHUTNEY

SHOP IT

1 pineapple, peeled, cored and finely cubed

6 cardamom pods, lightly crushed

5 sticks cinnamon

4 whole cloves

1 tsp turmeric

200g sugar

1 red chilli, finely sliced (optional)

PREPARE IT

Combine all the ingredients in a pan and cook for 20 minutes over a low heat, stirring well. Leave to cool. Keep refrigerated for up to 2 weeks.

PREPARE IT

Sauté the onion in a pan for 10 minutes until soft. Stir in the garlic, ginger and all the spices including the chilli and cook for 2 minutes. Add the tomato paste and cook for 2 minutes, then add the tomatoes, brown sugar, salt and pepper to taste and simmer for 15 minutes. Purée the mixture, return it to the pot and pour in the coconut milk. Bring to a boil, then remove from the heat.

Season the fish with salt, pepper and lemon juice, then pan-fry in the oil until lightly browned on both sides. Transfer it to a heat-proof dish and pour over the sauce. Heat through gently for 2 minutes. Serve topped with coriander and Pineapple Chutney.

Serves 6

KITCHEN NOTE
Any extra curry sauce can be frozen for later use.

KUKU PAKA WITH RAITA

KUKU PAKA

SHOP IT

20 skinless chicken thighs, bone in and halved

¼ cup sunflower oil

1 onion, chopped

3 sticks cinnamon

3 Tbsp cumin seeds

1 Tbsp whole cloves

3 cups peeled and finely chopped tomatoes

1 Tbsp tomato paste

4 Tbsp crushed garlic

1 ½ Tbsp grated fresh ginger

3 Tbsp ground coriander

2 Tbsp ground cumin

½ tsp turmeric

2 Tbsp chilli powder

salt

2 x 400ml cans coconut milk, heated

4 hard-boiled eggs, halved

PREPARE IT

Preheat the oven to 200°C.

Toss the chicken pieces in half the oil and roast until browned and cooked through. Fry the onion in the remaining oil with the cinnamon, cumin seeds and cloves. Add the tomatoes, tomato paste, garlic, ginger, coriander, ground cumin, turmeric and chilli powder. Cook over a medium heat for at least 20 minutes, adding a little water as necessary to prevent sticking or burning. Add salt to taste. The mixture is ready when the oil separates from the tomato mix. Add the heated coconut milk and bring to a boil, stirring all the time. Add the chicken pieces and simmer gently for 5 minutes.

Add the hard-boiled egg halves before serving with rice, rotis and raita.

Serves 8

RAITA

SHOP IT
1 English cucumber, peeled, seeded and roughly grated

1 tsp salt

1 cup plain yoghurt

salt and freshly ground black pepper

PREPARE IT
Toss the grated cucumber in the salt and allow to drain in a colander for 15 minutes. Squeeze out all the excess water, then mix the cucumber into the yoghurt. Taste before adding more salt and black pepper.

Makes 2 cups

Saffron, pistachios, turmeric, cardamom and all things nice enter our kitchen with sisters Shaheen and Faheen.

INDIAN KULFI ICE CREAM

If you have never eaten kulfi, a properly made kulfi, then you have never lived. Kulfi takes ice cream to a whole new level of heavenly delight. Dating back to 16th-century Mughal India, this rich, dense and creamy dessert can be flavoured with rose, mango, cardamom, saffron and pistachio. For an extra-fancy touch, serve a small square of Kulfi on one of grandma's dainty floral cake plates, if you remember where you packed them.

SHOP IT

1 x 380g can evaporated milk

1 x 385g can sweetened condensed milk

2 cups fresh cream

a generous pinch of saffron threads

½ tsp vanilla essence

½ tsp fresh cardamom seeds (no pods)

*½ cup roasted and chopped
    blanched almonds*

½ cup roasted and chopped pistachios

PREPARE IT

Freeze the evaporated milk overnight, then remove 1 hour before making the Kulfi.

Beat the evaporated milk and condensed milk together until fluffy. Beat the cream separately until it forms soft peaks and fold in half the saffron threads. Add the cream to the milk mixture and beat again. Stir in the vanilla essence and cardamom seeds, then beat until fluffy. Pour into a shallow plastic container, layering with the almonds and pistachios. Finally, top with more nuts and sprinkle over the remaining saffron threads, then freeze.

Cut into squares to serve.

Serves 8

AT THE FOREST BARBECUE

Who is the Tong Master?

Well, certainly not our guests. As with all the meals at the lodge, our guests have no role other than to stay put and eat. And then eat a little more. Sometimes we see our guests miming and gesticulating when they want to tell us something, because they are too nervous to open their mouths. Quite rightly so. We once counted that our guests can pop something in their mouths at up to 12 'events' a day. There is simply nothing better than feeding people.

At the barbecue in our lantern-lit forest, the mood, the food and the setting are seriously laidback. Just as a barbecue should be. Family dining is around tables decked with enamelware and dishcloths for napkins and groaning under Kenyan mezze starters. That is followed by grilled-to-order dishes from a choice (or combo) of beef, pork, chicken, fish and prawns, all served with roasted vegetables dressed in rocket, lemon and olive oil. And if you keep your eyes peeled through the trees into the darkness beyond, you are sure to see our resident hyena, ever hopeful, skulking around.

And for dessert? That's another story on another page.

STOKBROOD WITH KACHUMBARI

We love watching our Kenyan chefs wandering through the seated guests with bunches of stokbrood in their arms, like a bunch of beautiful lilies. But lilies certainly don't taste this good. Stokbrood, or stickbread, is just that. The best part is pulling it off the stick while still warm and dunking it into guacamole or hummus, or both. This is a nod to our South African roots and our chefs have mastered the pronunciation perfectly. Kachumbari, on the other hand, is the local version of a classic tomato, onion and chilli salsa. No Kenyan meal is complete without it.

STOKBROOD

SHOP IT
1 litre water

1.5kg cake flour

25g dried yeast

20g salt

1 cup olive oil

PREPARE IT
Combine all the ingredients, then knead for 10 minutes to form a dough. Cover and allow to prove until doubled in size.

Divide the dough into 20 equal-sized balls. Roll into 'ropes' about 30cm long. Wrap each length around an oiled cooking stick*. Place the end of the stick over glowing coals, rotating it so that the bread cooks evenly, but be careful not to burn. The bread should be ready in about 10 minutes. Eat immediately.

Makes 20

KITCHEN NOTE*
The quality of the stick is key. Look for something fairly straight and long (at least 1m) and about 2cm thick. Carve the bark off the point of the stick where you'll be attaching the dough.

KACHUMBARI

SHOP IT
6 tomatoes, julienned and pips removed

1 red onion, finely sliced

a bunch of coriander, finely chopped

1 chilli, finely chopped

olive oil to taste

lemon juice to taste

salt to taste

PREPARE IT
Mix the ingredients together and leave for an hour before serving.

Makes 2 cups

Head Chef Collins is proudly Kenyan, as is his merry band of cooks. A former boxer, soccer coach to the AFC and Arsenal fan, Collins is the cornerstone of our kitchen.

GRILLED RIB EYE
WITH CHIMICHURRI

SHOP IT

2 Tbsp olive oil

2 Tbsp lemon juice

2 Tbsp soy sauce

2 Tbsp Worcestershire sauce

2 stems fresh rosemary, destalked

a generous pinch of dried chilli flakes

freshly ground black pepper to taste

2 well-matured rib eye steaks, 3cm thick

Chimichurri:

*1 cup lightly packed chopped
  fresh parsley*

4 cloves garlic, minced

1 tsp salt

½ tsp freshly ground black pepper

½ tsp dried chilli flakes

2 tsp chopped fresh oregano

2 tsp minced onion

¾ cup vegetable oil

3 Tbsp red wine vinegar

3 Tbsp lemon juice

PREPARE IT

Mix together the olive oil, lemon juice, soy sauce, Worcestershire sauce, rosemary, chilli flakes and black pepper. Coat the steaks on both sides and chill for 8 hours, turning once.

Place all chimichurri ingredients in a blender or food processor and pulse until finely chopped, but not puréed.

Grill the steaks over the coals and spoon over chimichurri sauce to serve.

Serves 2

Chef Elias, nicknamed Chimichurri because he chimichurries around the kitchen, keeps us laughing no matter how high the pressure.

BARBECUE PORK BELLY WITH APPLE SAUCE

Kenyan pork is the unsung hero as beef has always stolen the limelight. Next time, skip the beef and go for the pork; you will be so glad you did. The best local ingredients are the foundation of Angama's cooking. Other than olive oil, balsamic vinegar, capers, quinoa and a couple of other staples, we are local all the way. And delightedly so.

PORK BELLY

SHOP IT

2kg boneless pork belly, with rind

½ lemon

salt

3 Tbsp olive oil

½ cup mango chutney

1 ½ cups water

1 cup red wine vinegar

2 large onions, thickly sliced

2 stalks celery, roughly chopped

2 carrots, chopped

10 cloves garlic, halved with skin on

½ cup grated ginger

a bunch of fresh thyme

2 cups white wine

3 cups chicken stock or water

PREPARE IT

Preheat the oven to 220°C.

Dry the pork belly and rub with the lemon, squeezing out the juice as you go. Leave for 10 minutes, then pat dry. Score the fat and sprinkle generously with salt and drizzle with oil. Rub into the skin.

Place the mango chutney, water and vinegar in a saucepan over a high heat, boil and whisk until smooth. Place the vegetables and herbs in a large, deep-sided roasting dish, add the chutney mixture and top with the pork, but ensure that the sauce does not wet the pork fat. Roast, uncovered, for 1½ hours, adding more water if necessary to prevent the liquid from drying up. Reduce the temperature to 190°C for another hour, adding 2 cups of white wine and more water to the pan. Reduce the temperature to 120°C and cook for another hour. Remove the pork from the roasting pan, and peel off the rind when cool enough to handle. Set the rind aside.

Reduce the pan scrapings until liquid has evaporated, and the vegetables are golden and sticky. Skim off the excess fat and add the three cups of stock or water to the pan, boiling and reducing to a good glaze. Strain the mango pan glaze and set aside until ready to serve.

Place the rind under the grill and cook until it puffs up. Serve with crispy rind pieces, mango pan glaze and cold apple sauce on the side.

APPLE SAUCE

SHOP IT

6 green apples, peeled, cored and cut into chunks

1 cup sugar

¼ cup lemon juice

PREPARE IT

In a covered pot, simmer the apple chunks in a little water with the lemon and sugar until soft and tender. Purée the apples using as much of the liquid to make a good thick purée. If necessary, add more sugar and lemon juice for a tangy sweet-sour apple flavour.

STEAK TAGLIATA
WITH ROCKET & PECORINO

When searching for the ultimate method of preparing Steak Tagliata, all roads led to Heston Blumenthal. Yes, it's a little more complicated than just grilling or pan frying the steak, slicing it and slathering it with rocket and shaved pecorino, but follow the steps carefully and you will be so glad you did.

SHOP IT

olive oil for cooking the steaks

2 x 300g sirloin steaks (or your choice of steak)

table salt flakes

½ cup olive oil

3 cloves garlic, peeled and bruised

6 sprigs fresh rosemary

2 strips lemon peel

juice of 1 lemon

salt and freshly ground black pepper

60g fresh rocket

balsamic crema

40g pecorino or parmesan shavings

PREPARE IT

Heat a heavy-bottomed frying pan over a high heat, then add a splash of olive oil and heat until it is smoking hot. Season the steaks with a little salt and place them in the smoking-hot pan for 15–20 seconds. Turn the steaks over and fry for a further 15–20 seconds. Repeat this, turning the steaks for 2½ minutes. Remove from the pan and allow to rest on a wire rack set over a plate to catch the juices.

Allow the frying pan to cool for 2 minutes then add the half a cup of olive oil, garlic, rosemary needles, lemon peel and lemon juice. Allow to infuse for 5 minutes. Strain this dressing through a sieve and sitr in any juices that have dripped from the steak.

Carve the steaks into 5mm-thick slices, season with salt and pepper and place on a serving dish. Spoon over half the dressing. Season the rocket leaves with salt and mix with the remaining dressing. Arrange the rocket leaves over the meat, drizzle with a good squeeze of balsamic crema and finish with pecorino or parmesan shavings and salt flakes.

Serves 4

KITCHEN NOTES

Chef Heston Blumenthal says: 'The key to this recipe is having the pan really, really hot before cooking the steak to ensure that it is well-coloured on the outside, but rare on the inside. If you prefer your meat more well done, cook it for longer but continue to turn it every 15–20 seconds for the duration of the cooking time.'

MEET THE CHEFS

Brenda Akinyi
salad chef

How many years cooking
2

Favourite AM recipe
Mara Caesar Salad

Favourite ingredient
Parmesan cheese

Collins Randiga
head chef

How many years cooking
17

Favourite AM recipe
Spinach Cannelloni, Chip
Seasoning

Favourite ingredient
Rocket oil

Corridon Sagala
baker

How many years cooking
12

Favourite AM recipe
Vanilla Fudge Ice Cream

Favourite ingredient
Chocolate

Daniel Katoli
kitchen assistent

How many years cooking
10

Favourite AM recipe
Shakshuka

Favourite ingredient
Feta

Elias Nanka
breakfast cook

How many years cooking
5

Favourite AM recipe
Chicken Pastilla

Favourite ingredient
Ginger and chilli

Evans Ondara
assistant head chef

How many years cooking
18

Favourite AM recipe
Tomato Soup

Favourite ingredient
Green onions

Hudson Khamadi Museni
picnic chef

How many years cooking
12

Favourite AM recipe
Roasted Butternut and Red
Onion Salad

Favourite ingredient
Mint

Jackson Saitoti
picnic chef

How many years cooking
1

Favourite AM recipe
Panzanella Salad

Favourite ingredient
Mint

James Nayok
chef

How many years cooking
12

Favourite AM recipe
Swahili Vegetable Curry

Favourite ingredient
Ginger, garlic, turmeric
and onions

John Lotaba
breakfast cook

How many years cooking
6

Favourite AM recipe
Spinach Cannelloni

Favourite ingredient
Salt and pepper

Joseph Nkoyo
senior chef

How many years cooking
24

Favourite AM recipe
Salted Caramel Brownies

Favourite ingredient
Chocolate

Katana Mweri
chef

How many years cooking
9

Favourite AM recipe
Indian Cauliflower Soup,
Lamb Pilaf

Favourite ingredient
All spices

Kina Kariankei
baker

How many years cooking
8

Favourite AM recipe
Maasai Honey Biscuits

Favourite ingredient
Chocolate

Kisemei Liaram
kitchen assistant

How many years cooking
3

Favourite AM recipe
Swahili Omelette

Favourite ingredient
Turmeric

Moses Koros
kitchen assistant

How many years cooking
15

Favourite AM recipe
Butter Chicken

Favourite ingredient
Turmeric

Musa Jacob Ezekiel
staff cook

How many years cooking
25

Favourite AM recipe
Swahili Vegetable Curry

Favourite ingredient
Curry and chilli

John Paaiyo Ole Kunani
staff cook

How many years cooking
7

Favourite AM recipe
Nyama Choma

Favourite ingredient
Nyama

SWAHILI CULINARY TERMS

Tafadali	Please	*Chai*	Tea	*Bitings*	Snacks
Asante	Thank you	*Maji*	Water	*Ugali*	Polenta
Niongeze tafadali	Some more please	*Barafu*	Ice	*Mandazi or Muhamri*	Doughnuts
Hiki ni kitamu sana	This is delicious	*Pombe*	Beer	*Kachumbari*	Tomato Salsa
Kiamsha kinywa	Breakfast	*Furahia!*	Cheers!	*Pili pili*	Chilli
Chakula cha mchana	Lunch	*Kuku*	Chicken	*Moto*	Hot
Chakula cha jioni	Dinner	*Nyama*	Meat	*Baridi*	Cold
Kahawa	Coffee	*Samaki*	Fish		

WHAT TO COOK